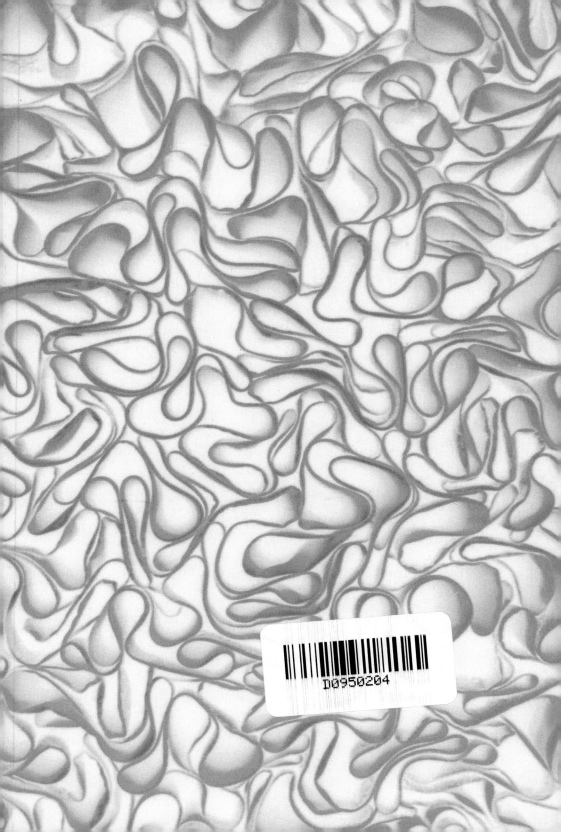

D0950204

THE SCARLET IBIS

ALSO BY SUSAN HAHN

Harriet Rubin's Mother's Wooden Hand

Incontinence

Confession

Holiday

Mother in Summer

Self/Pity

THE
SCARLET
IBIS

POEMS

SUSAN HAHN

NORTHWESTERN UNIVERSITY PRESS

EVANSTON, ILLINOIS

Northwestern University Press
www.nupress.northwestern.edu

Printed in the United States of America

10 9 8 7 6 5 4 3 2 1

ISBN-13: 978-0-8101-5183-3 (CLOTH)
ISBN-10: 0-8101-5183-9 (CLOTH)
ISBN-13: 978-0-8101-5184-0 (PAPER)
ISBN-10: 0-8101-5184-7 (PAPER)

LIBRARY OF CONGRESS CATALOGING-IN-PUBLICATION DATA

Hahn, Susan.
     The scarlet ibis / Susan Hahn.
         p. cm.
     ISBN 978-0-8101-5184-0 (pbk. : alk. paper) —
     ISBN 978-0-8101-5183-3 (cloth : alk. paper)
     I. Title.
PS3558.A3238S33 2007
811'.54—dc22
                                    2006039018

For Charlie

My friend must be a bird,
Because it flies!
Mortal my friend must be,
Because it dies!
Barbs has it, like a bee.
Oh, curious friend,
Thou puzzlest me!

—Emily Dickinson

CONTENTS

BIRD AND LADY

ACKNOWLEDGMENTS

Grateful acknowledgment is made to the editors of publications in which these poems, or versions of them, first appeared:

Boulevard: bird trick i, ii, iii, iv

Michigan Quarterly Review: lady trick i, ii, iii, iv

New England Review: Bird I, II, III, IV, V, VI, VII

Virginia Quarterly Review: Lady I, III, V, VI

This manuscript was conceived and completed with the assistance of a grant from the John Simon Guggenheim Memorial Foundation. My gratitude to the Foundation for its gift is unending.

THE SCARLET IBIS

BIRD

I

Almost extinct against
the deltas, it still appears
to startle eyes.
That flash of color a theater—
the backdrop, the stretched sky—
all wing and glide.
The bird arrives

who is leaving—
the one the Pharaohs took
to their tombs,
to the next world, the image

the god Thoth wore
as his head mask
when he recorded the worth
of a life. Whom I now tap
on his stiff shoulder

with a request—
last wish—ask
if he might take note
of us both.

bird trick i

A fake bird head
attached to a small bag
with concealed red fluid.
A knife able to shave thin
strips of paper—prove the keenness
of its edge. Draw the audience

gullible, the living bird
vulnerable. *Quick* tuck its soft head
under a wing to create
the sheltered fetal memory of being.
That constant of arriving. *Cut*

the bag with the blade.
Stain. The knife, your hand.
Never let loose the impulse,
consider the notion

of spreading it to the breathing
bird, the blood
would seem repulsive
upon its apparent restoration.

II

In the trees, in low bushes, among the reeds,
or on the ground, sits the Ibis
in its nest of sticks and stems—
its cavity lined with mud and dung.
Sits the Ibis on its eggs—
long legs folded
under loose webbed down.
Its statuesque neck reaches
the suggestion of otherworldliness,
enough to rival the god sun.
A burst of being aflame
with full life heat
underneath.

III

Flap and soar in unison,
with no voice, the joy in
the wing beat passing
down brilliant columns of flight,
strong thin-curved bills—
crescent moons reminding
the sun of its own twilight

dive into oblivion.
The bird forever
too beautiful, too tempting
to the slaughterer.

bird trick ii

No suspicion to attach
to the totally transparent
cage of thin nickel plate.
The bottom nothing
but a black sheet
supported on a wooden frame
with four feet. Four birds

needed. Two for the confectioner's
bag with its secret
pouch at the top into
which the birds visibly are dropped.
The mouth's pocket fastened
with fine wire. *Remember*

the usefulness of wire. And a gun

for the illusion of destruction—
a shot through the lower half
of the bag. Two birds hidden

in the hollow,

feet now sprung
into the cage
by means of a spring.

Spring sprung. *Chirp,*
it works.

All four birds
safe and sound.

IV

Caged, the bird is narrowed with stilted
legs and feathers of faded pink,
its bowed beak
out of proportion
to the rest of its pressed body.
It longs

for a nest where the river rises
to overflow. Not here,
in the city zoo,
where only an acrylic dream exists

of coastal marshes and inland plains
drenched with bushes of the burning
color, enough to hush, to stun
an observer bathed in drifting
gardens of hyacinths
and the hung-moon sky.
As if it all could be
with a placard attached—and is—

on a wire barrier that reads
GUARA RUBRA.
But there is no bird here
of that plumage, just a creature

jabbing at some garbage.

V

Wicker, wooden, metal bars,
gilt wire, tiered shapes, gingerbread,
and fretted carvings—swags
of simulated draperies, urns.
Mahogany with marquetry panels,
pagoda shaped with red lacquer,
rickrack braid, chrome,
unvarnished split bamboo,
plastic, fiberglass, cedar,
painted canopies entwined
with rustic vines and grapes.
Most safe for a fake

bird, less so for one with song
made to acclimate
to this life. Never
for the quiet Ibis
who stands its nature
in waters infested with
piranha fish.

bird trick iii

Better from the conjurer's point of view—
makes him seem more clever—
this cage has open sides and back.
Allows the audience to see right through
(or so they think they do).
       The innocent

top really an apartment where the bird is
placed—well ventilated, of course.
The bottom draws up and fastens
to it by means of a catch.
       There's always a catch,

especially necessary in a trick.
       There's always a trick,

this one with the center pole
apparently made to accommodate
a perch—really a guide—
(guides like to make themselves appear
apparent) for the false
(and are usually false)
top to slip down, the perch
being a loose slide, taking
the place of the one at the bottom.

If confusing to visualize,
just imagine the bird
in repose—hidden—
then exposed, hidden, hidden,
then exposed . . .

VI

The Scarlet Ibis is eating at my heart.

In every body crevice—nests
piled deep—its sweet eggs
hatch a destiny of beauty.
Wide-eyed, blunt-beaked, nails dulled,
it cuddles into my chest.
A soft survival between us.

The Scarlet Ibis is eating at my heart.

Bird of a silent lust
keeping to itself, flying
too close
to the indifference
of the sun,
its survival melts—
grey to pink to rose to red
to bruised scarlet
to black silhouette.

The Scarlet Ibis is eating at my heart.

Against the horn and claw and talon,
the tooth and fang and poison gland,
nocturnal monkey, rodent, snake—
who long ago gave up trying to lift
its backbone from the dust—

against a thousand skittering
things on branch and humus
and heap, it stands.

The Scarlet Ibis won't stop
eating at my heart.

Last love of mine,
it clings to me
as I to it,
until all our feathers are
world plucked.

bird trick iv

It's all about disappearance.

About a bird in a cage
with a mirror, a simple twist
on the handle at the side
that makes it come and go

at the magician's insistence.

It's all about innocence.
It's all about acceptance.
It's all about compliance.
It's all about deference.
It's all about silence.

It's all about disappearance.

VII

On the contour of feathers—
how they fan out to protect—
notice the tips
(a tip to the future),
black against the flared red

that tilts the world—
an overheated vertigo
that insists on our stare.
Against that fire

the black absorbs all light,
accepts the singe of the sun
as if it were a gift,
the way we accept
the recline into night.
The tips of the Ibis

missed at first glance return
in the soot hour, touching
a scab that will not disappear,
awake the nightmare—
that flash of recognition—
the arrow that zeroes
to the spot where sickness
begins. In the tomb mouth

Ibis-faced Thoth
weighs every heart
against the feather of truth,
which no heart can rival,
judges where to send next
the scaled soul,
writes it down with his reed pen—

Master Magician of the Bird Trick—

body finally at rest,
the tips of the Ibis
are concealed
in a crypt.

LADY

lady trick i

The lady lets the audience watch,
full stare—
they've paid a lot
to be voyeurs—
while she sits
on the chair. Moves

just halfway in. Keeps

legs apart. Smiles
at them—especially the men.
Throws her chest out,
while being bound—

arms in front, hands folded
like the good girl
in school who does what
she is told to do. Always

knows to carry a duplicate
length of rope
(and of self) concealed
next to her heart, watches
as that partition slides
away from their grins.
Should she find she can't

break free, loosen herself,
she cuts what binds—
cuts it quick—
with a sharp penknife
kept on the inside
pocket of her thin blouse.
Holds it tight between
her teeth. *Now*
released, she appears
in front of the screen.

Know someday she will
not escape.

I

It begins on a tip

of the ear in
reality or metaphor—
it doesn't matter.
The matter out

of which we're made more
determined than any life
guide shoved at us
by mother or by father.
What is this

condition? What causes it?
What are its symptoms?
How to diagnose it?
To treat it?

Treat it with fear.

lady trick ii

The lady lies in an iron cage.
Padlocks snapped shut on the door
at the top and the sides reinforce
that there's no way out.
No traps, no mirrors

used for this trick—
although a mirror would be nice,
for ladies like

to adjust their hair before
they vanish (haven't you
noticed this?). The screen
placed in front appears
for just ten seconds.
That's all it takes

to disappear (so far,
I've witnessed this
twice). Escape

is what the lady's after—
it's in her power. Although
the audience only applauds
the conjurer, which isn't fair,
for the lady has pressed hard

through rubber bars at the back,
rolled herself onto a narrow leaf
table that drops her
down to the floor.
No one sees how fast
she gets up, runs
through the slit

curtain to the back
to vomit, then
to the mirror to touch
her face, her hair, make sure
she's still here.

II

Here, the blood vessels contract
in quick successive rhythms.
It is so cold on the vermilion border
of old—that tangled mass
of arteries and veins a regimented mess.
There is no surprise and yet

I cannot get used to this
underside of flesh—its
ridges, valleys, pits.
The aged cells

at the top flake off and leave
a minute path of familiarity,
but more and more
the skin wounds burst
into an odd territory
with uninvited effects—
up from the broken

heart to the dermis to
the epidermis there is a redundancy
of growth. An insanity

of divisions—a war being waged.
Troops on both sides aim and kill
while I stand in the middle, stare
at the site—the sight of the foreigner
in the mirror.

lady trick iii

Lay the lady
on a block of wood
in a fanciful dress—
all folds and drape.
How lost she is
in the bright
fabric. Perfect

to keep the flesh hidden,
swathed and buried deep.
When the axe hits
hard on her back

she can relax,
cross her legs on the rod
between her knees.
No one can see

the corset with the iron
support, the huge notch—
how it engages the blade.
A simple sideshow
attraction, old as humans
dressed in satin charade.

All that's needed is a lady,
a costume, and a room.

III

On the high curve of the ear,
outside the head's whir and whirl,
on the flesh without bone—
yet somewhat tough and elastic—
is the singed tip. Sick

wing without any ambition
to fly close to the sun, none-
theless done in by it.
Its relentless glare

on a body overstaying
its welcome
on the planet crust—
a body which should have been
already buried and reduced to ash—
tossed back

into the atmosphere.
Too much consciousness
inflames the diseased

questions (*Who will tell
my story? Can thought travel
without the skin vessel?*),
creates a soot that blows back

into the face, which sucks it in
to become the smudged
mind. The person

who once sat next to me—
held my small hand with tight care—
has become the vague one
I am sitting in. Here

lies the sore
that does not heal,
the one that will
become the end
of the story
of the low flight journey.

IV

No skinned knee or other ordinary
scrape, rather an odd fight here
against a bully with multiplying
angles of reproach—
canny and so self-
involved, so self-assured, dis-
allowing an Ouroboros spin
of destruction, of rebirth

      (of hope)

not a battle to be settled
by some outside jury—
sky high or on its belly.
What's gone awry is a personal
dispute over territory—a body.
A war of cut and paste

      (of hope)

goes on with a kindergarten kind
of naïveté—a ripped picture
of permanence rushed
home to mother waiting, waiting
at the door. There was a time

      (of hope)

she was there, remember. *Remember*
says the surgeon never to sleep
on the wound. It makes
the inflammation angrier.
That lonely patch sewn in
needs to convince its neighbors

      (of hope)

to believe it is the one
to take over the region

      (of hope)

believe in its religion.

V

The body not yet anointed with coniferous resins,
not yet packed with wads of linen,
just some sterile pads of gauze and adhesives
to keep the skin bound and grounded
to this space, not yet ready

to slip through the corridor, the chamber,
the great hall, where the Ibis lies bandaged
next to the mummy with its mouth cut
so it can still ask
for *some thing* if it has cause,
not yet *this* body with its compression

tape held tight, the wound
where the dug scab once lived—
the crater where I now sleep
curled around the fevered wings
and quiver of a bird with black tips.

VI

Hunting for the margins of the wound,
trying to get past the rancid place
to a paradise of garden
where the ancient tree remains
green and fresh—serves as a canopy
for the monk and his piper—
I found only the sacrifice

of sheep intestines (or was it silk
thread or, perhaps, the lesser nylon?)
attempting to hold the marked
land together. My body
a haunting from which
I could not find the latch

to open, crawl out, inhale, take back
the breaths of *WHEN*. Though I imagined
and reimagined them—the times
that were and would
not come again. So I returned

to the wound and began
to bury myself there, remembering
the stunned fingers, how they touched
the weeping skin. Those lost

eyes of my mother and her mother—
the look of them. Over

and over again.

lady trick iv

Queen of Knives, Talking Skull, The Bodiless,
always the illusion of something other.
There, then not. Lover

of mirrors and traps, the romance
of levitation, making the audience
rise to all occasions. Lady

in the wooden box who vanishes
and comes back from seen
nothingness. Magician's assistant, victim,

necessary vision for the trick,
surgeon's patient, payment,
his creation without whom he
could not exist.
Bird in a cage
whose song entertains,
then is silenced. Dictator's

mistress who signed the contract
not to rival or reveal
any secret.

BIRD
AND
LADY

Prologue

LADY:
The Scarlet Ibis has come to live with me.
It sits next to my chair,
lets me lift its wing, touch
its black tips.
I know it wants

to tell me things,
but it has no voice.
I beg it to anyway.
I have a voice but little
left to say. I say

come close, press your beak
to the opening
of my bandaged ear,
let me hear you
breathe, have your breath

and I will write of it.

I

BIRD:
I come from a place surrounded by water,
the soil loamy.

LADY:
I come from a place similar.
My ancestors born in the town
of Dachau. Once
an artists' colony. Once
a place of beauty.

(It points its beak away
as if there's nothing more to say.
I look at the quarter moon adrift
in the sky—a beak so far away.)

WHYWHYWHY
do you wander from *here*?

(It looks shocked but returns
to my ear.)

BIRD [*sadly*]:
What exactly is it
that you want from me?

LADY:
I want. I want
poetry.

II

BIRD:
Is it time for the trick?

LADY:
(I see a wry smile in its eyes
and feel sick.)

The trick?

BIRD:
O please, it's not that you don't know of it.
[*pause*]
The part where we disappear.
The part where we *seem* to die.
You forget?
[*pause*]
You did ask me to be
here while you write
your manuscript.
And this is what I suggest.
The Trick.

LADY:
You're impatient.
[*pause*]
You're rushing it.
The answer is,
no trick—
at least, not yet.

III

LADY:
(I'm holding the bird
too tight—too much pleasure—
and out falls a feather.
The bird looks me in the eye,
as if this were familiar.)

BIRD:
A plume for your hat?
Perhaps
to decorate your sweater,
its collar?

LADY:
No. No, I wouldn't do that,
at least not now.
[*pause*]
Now, not ever.

BIRD:
Why? Do you care?
Or just pretend
for the sake of your pen?

LADY:
No. No, some of my family disappeared.
[*pause*]
Ask my grandmother, unlatch

the locket on her stone, stare
at her eyes sick with a fear
that goes beyond the graveyard.

BIRD:
I get it! *This Is The Trick!*
To merge us into one and say
we're not just similar,
but the same.
[*pause*]
It sounds a bit insane.

LADY:
Yes, like my grandmother.

IV

LADY:
On a hill with a view of the Alps,
a marketplace for gathering—
bucolic and picturesque, a residence
of kings, a summer palace—
her father, a painter, made it
his home until called to a war
he did not own, never
to return. His legacy
the stains left on his canvas—
her mother, brothers, sister, and her
waiting there for his kiss.

BIRD:
Sorry. *Too romantic.*
[*pause*]
The colony became a munitions
factory while she was growing up—
your timing a bit off.

LADY:
True. I just wanted it to sound—

BIRD:
More poetic?

LADY:
Yes.

[*pause*]
She never spoke of any of it—
the town, its beauty, her family.
I only know that was where
they were when they were
lost to her.

BIRD:

In the swamp there are always predators.
One can survive if frozen in fear.
[*laughs*]
How one stays, nearly always a cliché.

LADY:

The two of us would stand
immobile by the kitchen window.
She held my hand so tight
whenever anyone was late—
muttering just one word
death
first in broken English,
then in Yiddish,
until each rose up
the three flights.
[*pause*]
Then, she'd quiet.

V

LADY:
They wore hats—
my mother and her mother—
hats with feathers.
It was the '40s.
It was the '50s.

BIRD:
Please, no excuses.

LADY:
It was a time when people *dressed,*
even if they had little money.
How their faces brightened
with those small bursts
atop their heads.
I do remember a startling
[*smiles*]
red.

BIRD:
It isn't funny.

LADY:
You're right. Of course.
Sorry,
that was unfortunate.
Incorrect.

But the truth is,
three months ago
I wouldn't have
felt that.

BIRD:
Three months ago you didn't know
that you were sick—
or, for that matter,
that I did exist.

LADY:
I was stopped by your picture
in a book.
[*pause*]
Your black tips.
Put down my pen and touched
the sore.

BIRD:
No one will ever believe that.

LADY:
I don't care.
[*pause*]
It will be our secret.

BIRD:
Like lovers—are we?
Quite a notion.
Eventually found out.
Our extinction.

VI

LADY:
It became a godless soil, ashes
dumped into the river, the ponds,
yet on the same grounds
an angora rabbit breeding
farm was found
(as if a view from a petting zoo)
along with gardens filled with exotic
herbs and spices.
[*pause*]
In Sleeping Room One there
were 90 beds in 30 three-tiered bunks
(the piling of bodies beginning
there).

BIRD:
You went and saw?
A tourist dressed in shorts,
returning home with such reports?

LADY:
No. Pictures in a book I found.

BIRD:
Ah, pictures, again.
[*pause*]
Another kind of fear frozen.

LADY:

It's what I have to go on. *To go on*
I spend my time mostly sitting
in one chair, my fingers tracing the edges
of the bandages—the radio's repetitive
news tightening around me.
[*pause*]
My grandfather would sit for hours—
so quiet—smoking cigarettes.

BIRD:

His lungs singed
by their black tips?

LADY:

Yes.
[*pause*]
She'd scream at him
to fix it.

BIRD:

Who? Fix What?

LADY:

My grandmother. Everything—
the sink, the toilet, the unending
stink. She could never get free of it.
[*pause*]
Sometimes he would read the Old Testament—
stopping often to look *up*.
He had studied to be a rabbi

in that soil gone to rot.
Here, he worked in a kosher
butcher shop.

VII

BIRD:
Once, I got lost,
flew over that place,
saw the tourists in their wrinkled pastels.
The memorial between the barracks—
the bronze barbed-wire figures twisted
to torment, the wedge-shaped
building, its barred entrance,
the strip of marble extending
through a hole in the roof,
the menorah resting at the top.
I felt weak
and landed on it.
No one could believe what they saw—
me resting there—
so they pretended not to see.
[*pause*]
I stood for much more than a moment,
watched all those bare legs
move from spot to spot,
thought how much I needed
to find a way back
to my flock.

LADY:
And you expect me to believe this?

BIRD:
As I do you
[*pause*]
and do not.

VIII

LADY:
My mother wore a red suit—

BIRD:
Stop.

LADY:
Why?

BIRD:
Because it's just not appropriate.
I am not
her metaphor, she mine, or I yours.
I am not
[*pause*]
the messenger.

LADY:
Everything is metaphor
[*pause*]
or messenger.
It's how we're able to remain sane
here.

BIRD:
Don't use me for your poetry.
I'm tired of being mummified,
[*pause*]

of being bound in tombs
next to the dead
as if I could lead them
to an unknown
I do not know.
[*pause*]
Tired of all the picking
at my feathers—human hands
busying themselves
over my bones. I have little
to show for it. Beauty
[*pause*]
always a sad-end story.

IX

LADY:
I looked under the bandages.
The skin has evened
but is still an insistent red.
[*pause*]
How deep the scar
in scarlet weeps.

BIRD:
I am *not* your scar.
[*pause*]
You are.

LADY:
I believe she chose a red suit because—

BIRD:
Enough! I want to fly away, *away*
from all of this.
[*pause*]
From what you make
of me. Again, I am not
your *poetry*.

LADY [*sadly*]:
You are. No matter how far—

BIRD:
And no *bird trick* can fix it.
There is no *trick*
[*pause*]
to get her back.

LADY [*softly*]:
Yes,
I now know that.

X

LADY:
Where would you go from here—
if you could go anywhere?

BIRD:
The Garden of Perfect Brightness
beside The Lake of Happiness.
There, among the little valleys,
lotus and chrysanthemums,
I'd pause—
watch the moon, compose
[*smiles*]
poems.

LADY:
You'd think of me. I'd be your muse!

BIRD:
You are really confused.
[*pause*]
I want peace—away from all that's human.
All that's vile. All that's silly.

LADY:
So do I. Like you. Like me.
We could be each other's simile.

BIRD:
I do not *like* you.

LADY:
I do not *like* me.

XI

BIRD:
Go to the garden—the one *you* mentioned
in an earlier section.
Find your own prayer,
your own meditation.
I am not who will weigh your soul
in the end.
I am not
your seer, your guide, your scribe,
your friend. I will not be
locked in your tomb.
[*pause*]
Why she chose red
for her final journey—bound herself
in that color—is a question
no one can answer.
[*pause*]
When all the bandages are removed
and you look into the mirror,
see yourself for who you are.

LADY:
Who am—

BIRD:
Don't *ask* me that anymore.
[*pause*]
I've said this before.

[*pause*]
I'm tired. Tired
of your history. *Of all*
of you. Of what you do
to yourselves and to each other.
[*pause*]
Of what you've done to me.

LADY:
I've done nothing—

BIRD:
That's what they *all* say.

LADY:
O I know. I do agree.

BIRD:
Shut up. Shut up.
[*pause*]
Please.
[*pause*]
I'm leaving now. Going. *Going*
to fly away. No more
for you to use.

LADY:
O muse.

BIRD [*softly*]:
You'll be OK.
[*pause*]

So will I.
In the end
we both will die
and leave this struggle
to other creatures
now being born
to wander between
earth and sky.

Epilogue

BIRD:
. . . until all that live—
all that move, act
by instinct, all
who think, believe
they know all
answers—
are extinct.

ABOUT THE AUTHOR

Susan Hahn is a poet, a playwright, and the editor of *TriQuarterly* magazine. She is the author of six previous books of poetry and the recipient of many awards for her poems, including a Guggenheim Fellowship in 2003. The *Chicago Tribune* named her fourth book, *Holiday,* and her fifth book, *Mother in Summer,* among the best books of 2002. Her first play, *Golf,* premiered in 2005.

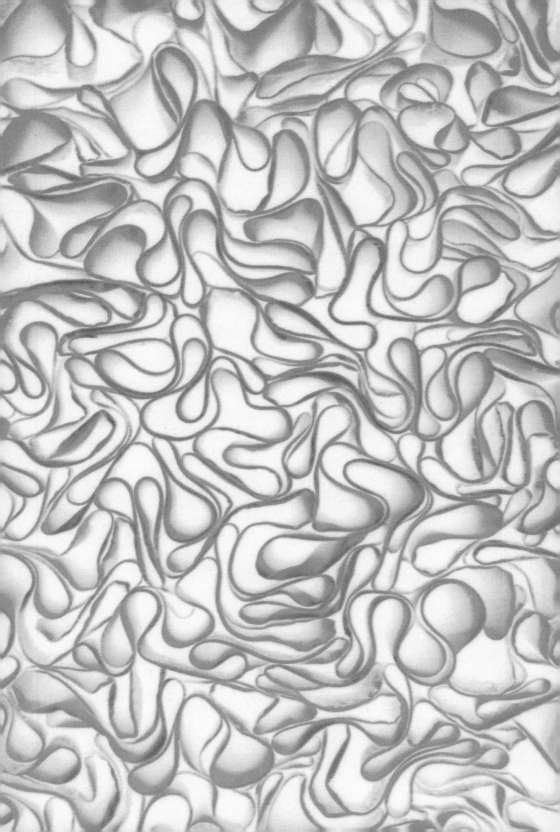